AN OVERVIEW OF THE LEGAL SERVIES AUTHORITIES ACT 1987

VOLUME 2, ISSUE 2 OF BRILLOPEDIA

P. ISHWARYA

Contents

Preface

"Start writing, no matter what. The water does not flow until the faucet is turned on".

-Louis L'Amour

Hundreds of students and professors are contributing their work to Brillopedia, we are here to provide ample information about Law and Contemporary issues. Our aim is to provide a platform for today's generation to express their views and ideas on law and contemporary law.

Publication

This research paper is published in volume 2, issue 2 of Brillopedia

Author

P. Ishwarya

Enter Caption

CHAPTER ONE

Abstract

To promote equal distribution of justice among the people, the France and Britain governments introduced free legal services in their countries to the competent person. Based on this idea, the Indian government through the 42nd amendment Act inserted Article 39A in the constitution of India, to provide equal opportunity to access the law to the needy people. The effect of insertion of Article 39A, the Legal Service Authorities Act 1897came into existence. The government also constituted certain authorities and committees such as central authority, state authority and district authority under the act. This legislation also contains provisions regards Lok Adalat, criteria for obtaining free legal service and so on. The important function of the authority is to conduct legal aid programs and awareness at universities, rural areas and schools etc. Every year 9th of November is celebrated as National Legal Service Day. As per Article 14 of the Indian constitution, all are equal before the law.

"Law without Justice is a wound without a cure".

CHAPTER TWO

Introduction

The legal services authorities act was introduced in the year 1987 by the parliament of India. The purpose of the act is to provide free legal services to people with certain conditions.

<u>Features of the Act</u>

1. To provide free legal service to the people, the government constituted the legal service

authority at the central level, state level and District level.

2. The Act have 30 sections and seven chapters.

3. For the central level the national legal services authority was constituted under chapter II Section 3 of the act .

4. Under chapter III of the act deals with legal service authorities for the state and District levels.

5. This Act also contains provisions for Lok Adalat.

CHAPTER THREE

Preliminary

1. Section 1 deals with short title, extent and commencement.
    2. Important definitions under section 2

a.   The term 'case' denotes suit or proceedings.

   aa) central authority is also known as the national legal service authority under the act.

   aaa) The court is defined as any civil, criminal, revenue court and tribunals.

   h) state authority is defined as state legal service authority mentioned under the act.

CHAPTER FOUR

The National Legal Services Authority

3. Section 3

The national legal service Authority is comprised of the chief justice of India, other judges and members. After consultation with the chief justice of India, the judges and other members including the secretary was appointed.

The authority also has other officers and employees for performing functions mentioned under the Act. The fund for administrative expenses may be taken from the consolidated fund.

The salary and allowances of such officers and employees may be determined by the central government after consultation with the chief justice of India.

4. Section 3A of the Act talks about the Supreme Court legal services committee.

- The committee includes a judge of the apex court and other members. The qualification for such members will be determined by the central government.
- The committee also have a secretary who is appointed by the chief justice of India.
- To perform other functions the officers and employees will also be appointed. The salary and allowance for such employees and officers may be determined by the central government.

5. Section 4 talks about the functions of the central authority.

1) The first function of the authority is to make policies and principles regarding legal service.

2) To conduct legal aid camps.

3) To promote settlement through Alternative Dispute Resolutions.

4) The authority also performs fund allocation functions for the state and district authorities.

5) one of the most important functions is to monitor the legal service committee and other legal organizations.

6) To ensure the duties given under Part IVA of the Indian constitution.

These are some of the important functions performed by the central authority under the act.

6. Section 5 The authority has to co-ordinate with governmental and non-governmental agencies to perform the functions given under the act.

CHAPTER FIVE

State legal services Authority

7. Section 6 talks about state legal services authority.

- The authority is embodied by the chief justice and other judges of the high court. The other judges may include either retired or serving judges of the high court.

- The members and secretary for such authority may be appointed after consultation with the chief justice of the High court.

- The authority also has officers and other employees to perform the functions mentioned under the act.

- The fund for administrative expenses shall be taken from the consolidated fund of the concerned state government.

- The salary and allowances for employees and officers shall be determined by the state government in consultation with the chief justice.

- The orders and decisions of the authority came into enforce only with the approval of the secretary.

8. Section 7 deals with functions of state authority.

- To provide legal services to the people and to conduct legal aid programs.

9. Section 8 To perform the functions given under the act the authority has to coordinate with some agencies, universities etc.

10. Section 8A like the central government, the State government also has a high court legal services committee.

- It comprises judges of the High court and other members. The committee also has a secretary who is appointed by the chief justice.
- To perform other functions given under the act, employees and officers will also be appointed.

11. Section 9 for the regional level the District legal service authority is established by the state government.

- The authority comprises the District Judge and other members. The secretary for such authority may also be appointed by the state authority in consultation with the chairman i.e district judge.

- For administrative expenses, the fund may be allotted from the consolidated fund of the state. Like central and state authorities, the district authority also has employees and officers for performing functions mentioned under the act.

12. Section 10

- The functions of the district authority is to conduct Lok Adalat at the regional level and to coordinate activities with the other committee.

13. Section 11 The authority has to coordinate with other agencies to perform the functions given under the act.
14. Section 11A Taluk Legal services committee

- The committee is embodied by the judicial officers and other members. The judicial officer will also act as ex-officio chairman for such a committee.
- It also has officers and employees to perform other functions of the act
- The fund for administrative expenses is given from the district legal aid fund with the approval of the district authority.

15. Section 11B deals with the function of the taluk legal service committee.

CHAPTER SIX

Entitlement to legal services

16. Section 12

The criteria for legal service are given under the section.

1. Person from scheduled caste or tribes

2. A person became a victim because of human trafficking or beggar.

3. A person defined under section 2 of clause (i) of the persons with disabilities (Equal opportunities, protection of rights and full participation) Act 1995.

4. Due to mass disasters, ethnic, violence, and flood, those who become victims will also right to get legal service under the act.

5. This act also provides legal service to a woman, child and a person in custody of a protective home.

6. if a person's income is below nine thousand rupees per year also has the right to get legal service and for supreme court cases, it may vary.

17. Section 13 one can be entitled to legal service if such a person comes under the category mentioned under section 12 of the Act.

CHAPTER SEVEN

Finance, Accounts and Audit

18. Section 14

- To perform the given function under the act the central government allot a sum of money to the central authority to do that work.

19. Section 15

- The fund allotted to the central authority, by the central government is called National Legal Aid Fund. It includes donations received by the central authority under the act.
- This fund may utilize for services provided to people by the legal service committee of the Supreme Court and to meet other expenses under the act also.

20. Section 16

- The state authority also has a state legal aid fund to perform the given function in the act.

21. Section 17

- Like central and state authorities the district authority also maintains the District Legal Aid fund to do the work mentioned in the act.

Lok Adalats
22. Section 19

- Except for the central authority, the other authority and committees given under the act must conduct Lok Adalats periodically to dispose of the cases pending before the court.

23. Section 20 is concerned with the cognizance of cases by Lok Adalat.

- If both parties agree, the dispute may settle through Lok Adalat.
- The Lok Adalat must follow certain principles such as justice, fair play and equity during the time of settlement.

24. Section 21 Award

- An award made by the Lok Adalat should be final and binding on the parties. Either of the parties cannot file an appeal for the same case.

25. Section 22

- The power of the Lok Adalat is given under the section.
- Like the civil court, the Lok Adalat also have the power to summon and examine the witness.

Pre-litigation conciliation and settlement

- Under the chapter, we are gonna discussed permanent Lok Adalat. Section 22A 22B, 22C, 22D, 22E deals with such provision.
- Either the central or state authority by giving notification may establish permanent Lok Adalat. It comprises the judge, not below the rank of the district judge and other persons.

CHAPTER NINE

Jurisdiction

The permanent Lok Adalat settles a dispute which is compoundable and the property has a monetary worth of less than ten lakh rupees. it need not follow the procedure given under the code of civil procedure,1908 but it has to follow the principle of natural justice. When an award is made through the Permanent Lok Adalat, it cannot be further challenged in any other court.

CHAPTER TEN

Suggestion & Conclusion

<u>Suggestion</u>

1. Free Legal services should also provide to third-gender people.

<u>Conclusion</u>

The government introduced many laws and schemes for the people's welfare but did it really reach the people? Still many of them do not aware of these kinds of legislation. The government should take effective measures to change such a situation.